621
384
01899

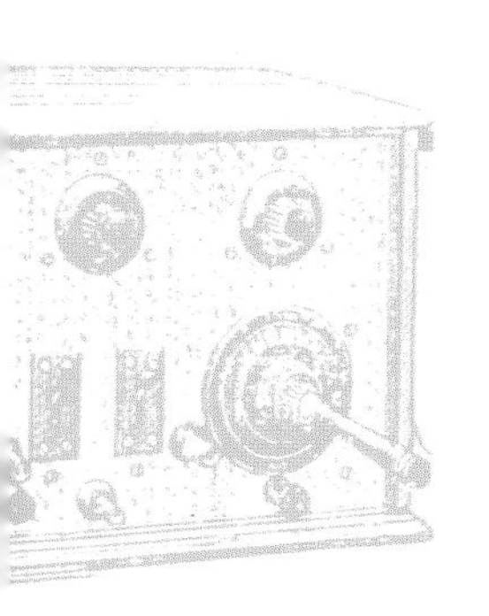

Science Discoveries

GUGLIELMO MARCONI

and Radio

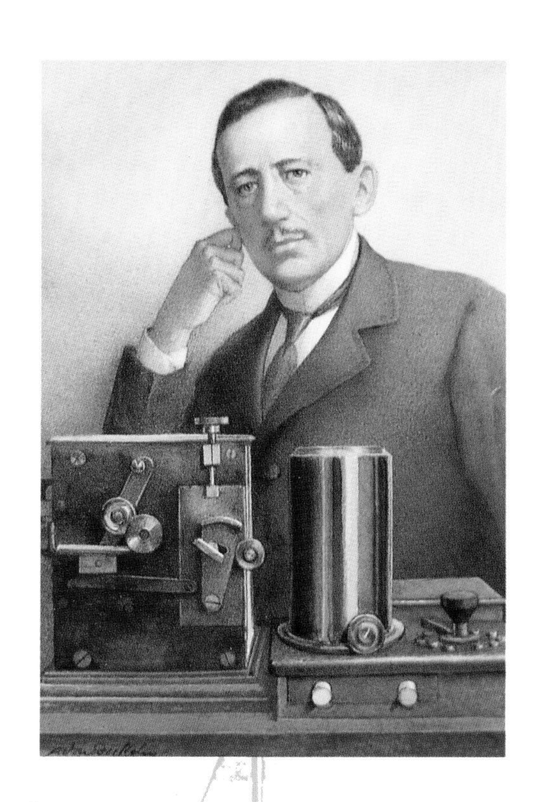

Steve Parker

Belitha Press

First published in Great Britain in 1994 by
Belitha Press Limited
31 Newington Green, London N16 9PU

Copyright © Belitha Press Limited 1994

Text © Steve Parker 1994

Illustrations/photographs copyright © in this format by Belitha Press Limited 1994
All rights reserved. No part of this book may be reproduced or utilised in any form or by any means, electronic or mechanical, including photocopying, recording or by any information storage and retrieval system, without permission in writing from the Publisher.

ISBN 1 85561 231 3
Typeset by Chambers Wallace, London

Printed in China for Imago

British Library Cataloguing in Publication data for this book is available from the British Library

Acknowledgements

Photographic credits:
Archive für Kunst und Geschichte, Berlin 23 left
E.T. archive 14 top, 22 bottom
Mary Evans Picture Library 13 bottom, 16 top, 18 top, 23 right
GEC Marconi 7 left and right, 12 bottom, 14 bottom, 19 bottom, 20 top, 24 top
Robert Harding Picture Library 27 top and bottom
Hulton Deutsch Collection 13 top, 20 bottom, 24 centre and bottom, 25 bottom, 26 bottom
Image Select/Ann Ronan Picture Library 5 top and bottom, 6, 15 top
Mansell Collection 8, 12 top, 17, 21 bottom
Retrograph archive, London/Martin Breese 22 top, 26 top
Science Museum, London 19 top
Science Photo Library/Dr Doug Johnson 4

Cover montage images supplied by Mary Evans Picture Library, GEC Marconi, Mansell Collection and Image Select/Ann Ronan Picture Library

Artwork: Tony Smith 9, 10/11, 18/19; Rodney Shackell 6, 15, 17, 21, 25
Editor: Rachel Cooke
Designer: Andrew Oliver
Picture researcher: Juliet Duff
Specialist adviser: John Booth
Thank you to GEC Marconi for their advice and co-operation

Contents

These dishes are part of the VLA Radio Telescope in New Mexico, USA. There are 27 in total, each 25 metres across. They pick up radio waves produced by gigantic bodies deep in space, such as quasars and pulsars, to reveal the secrets of the universe.

Introduction

Every day, in almost every way, we depend on **radio waves** – usually without realizing. In addition to normal radio broadcasts, radio waves are used in radio controlled devices, television broadcasts, mobile phones, **satellite communications**, **radar** and radio-navigation systems, weather forecasting, **radio-astronomy telescopes**, and many other ways.

Less than one hundred years ago, none of this existed. Telegraphs and telephones could send messages long distances, but only when linked by wires.

From about 1895 an Italian scientist, Guglielmo Marconi, carried out experiments using radio waves for communication. The invisible waves travelled through the air. Since the pieces of equipment were not joined by wires, it was known as "wireless communication".

Stage by careful stage, Marconi made his equipment more powerful. He sent radio messages farther. By 1920 radio circled the globe, and the first radio stations were broadcasting programmes to the public. Then TV arrived, and radar, and many other uses for radio. For Marconi, it all began in an attic room in his family villa near Bologna, Italy.

Chapter One

Early Influences

Marconi's work would not have been possible without the earlier contributions of several other scientists. In Italy in 1800, Alessandro Volta (1745-1827) made an electricity-producing **cell** – what we would call the first **battery**. It was an exciting discovery. Scientists such as Hans Oersted (1777-1851), André Ampère (1775-1836), Michael Faraday (1791-1867) and Joseph Henry (1797-1878) were soon experimenting with the **electric current** it produced.

During these experiments, they discovered links between **magnetism** and electricity. For example, an electric current flowing through a wire creates a **magnetic field** around the wire. If the current flowing constantly changes, it also produces an electric current in another wire nearby with no physical connection.

This early research paved the way for electric motors, generators, **transformers**, loudspeakers, telephones and many other devices now in everyday use.

Volta (above) discovered that certain combinations of metals and chemicals made electricity. His device became known as the voltaic pile – the first battery. He demonstrated it to Napoleon I (below).

James Clerk Maxwell proposed that various types of rays, including light, were forms of electromagnetic waves.

Invisible Waves

How were electricity and magnetism linked? Scottish scientist James Clerk Maxwell (1831-79) was a theorist. He did few experiments, but he thought long and hard about the problem, and used mathematics and the principles of physics as his tools.

In 1864 Maxwell predicted that changes in the amount of electricity in a wire should send out "waves" through the air, like waves of water rippling across a pond. These waves consisted of magnetism and electricity, and were known as **electromagnetic waves**. People could not see or feel or touch them, but they could be detected by electrical equipment.

Maxwell also proposed that light rays were a visible form of electromagnetic waves. He suggested that all electromagnetic waves travelled at the speed of light. These predictions were shown to be true (see panel).

Electromagnetic Waves

- Electromagnetic waves are a form of energy. They spread from their source in a combined electrical-magnetic form. They can pass through air, many liquids such as water, and even through the nothingness of space.
- We cannot hear electromagnetic waves, or smell or taste them. But we can see some of them. Light rays are one type of electromagnetic wave.
- We can also feel some of them. Heat is another type of electromagnetic wave.
- Radio waves are another type, as are X-rays and microwaves.
- All electromagnetic waves travel at the speed of light, that is, 299,792 kilometres each second (186,291 miles per second). They could go seven and a half times around the Earth in one second.
- Electromagnetic waves are measured by their **wavelength**. This is the distance from a point on one wave, such as the peak, to the same point on the next wave.
- The diagram shows the range or spectrum of electromagnetic waves, with some of their wavelengths.

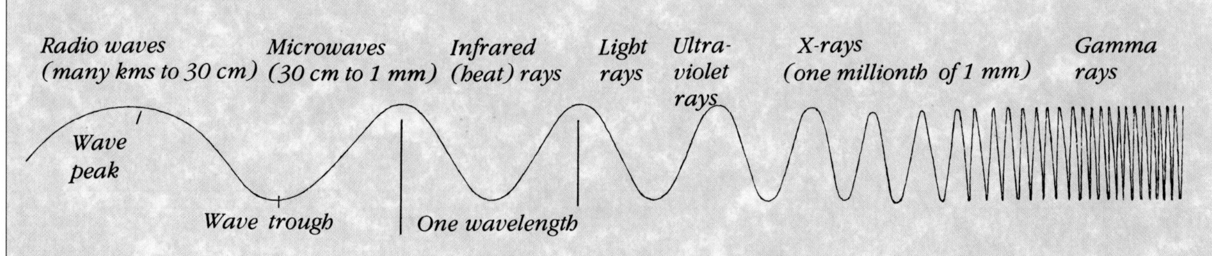

A Comfortable Childhood

Ten years after Maxwell's predictions, on 25 April 1874, a baby boy was born in Bologna, Italy. Guglielmo Marconi spent his first weeks at his family's town house, the Palazzo Marescalchi, in the Piazza San Salvatora.

Guglielmo's father, Guiseppe Marconi, was a wealthy landowner. He loved the countryside and was known as a keen businessman. His mother, Signora Marconi, was formerly Annie Jameson, whose Scottish family lived in Ireland. The two had met in Bologna while Annie was a music student, and married in 1864.

The baby Guglielmo had a nine-year-old brother Alfonso, and also an elder half-brother, Luigi, by his father's previous marriage.

Life was comfortable for the Marconis. Soon after Guglielmo's birth, they moved to their country house, the Villa Griffone at Pontecchio, near Bologna. In what became a settled yearly routine, they lived at the villa with its beautiful gardens in summer. In the harsh Bologna winter, the whole family would move to Florence or Leghorn, for milder weather.

This family photograph shows five-year-old Guglielmo with his mother and older brother Alfonso. In the background is the family home, Villa Griffone.

The Work of Hertz

German scientist Heinrich Hertz developed equipment to send and detect electromagnetic waves during the 1880s, transmitting waves over several metres.

Maxwell's mathematics said that the electromagnetic waves would be sent out by an electric current which flowed one way and then the other, changing direction or oscillating, very rapidly.

Normal mains electricity has a **frequency** of 50 or 60 Hertz, named after the scientist. We call it AC or **alternating current**. It changes direction 100 to 120 times each second – twice its frequency.

To produce radio waves, electricity needed to oscillate much faster – thousands or millions of times each second! Hertz built equipment to do this, using devices such as **induction coils**, that produce rapid, strong bursts of electricity.

Not a Good Boy

Guglielmo had his own tutors (teachers), but his schoolwork was not remarkable. He said later: "I was not a good boy." He could be stubborn and sometimes got into trouble. However, he showed two parts of his personality that helped in later life. He could concentrate hard for long periods. He also got on well with people, and persuaded them to believe in what he was doing.

From 14, Guglielmo was sent to school and it was then he became fascinated by chemistry and physics, especially electricity.

Inspired by Hertz

By the age of 20, Marconi spent all his time on science. His father provided money, but he was not keen on his son's obsession. In 1894, the Marconi brothers holidayed in the Italian Alps. Marconi had read about the work of Heinrich Hertz (1857-94), who had recently died. Hertz had sent so-called "**etheric**" (electromagnetic) waves over distances of several metres, without wires, and detected them.

While trying to sleep in the hotel one night, Marconi had an idea. In the telegraph and telephone, messages were sent as electrical signals along wires. Could the electromagnetic waves carry messages as signals, in the same way? He decided to work on the idea of "wireless telegraphy" until he succeeded.

Marconi worked long hours in his attic rooms, keeping the doors locked even when he was inside. His father remarked that it was like a state of siege. His mother was more supportive, even going so far as to get up in the middle of the night to witness her son's first success.

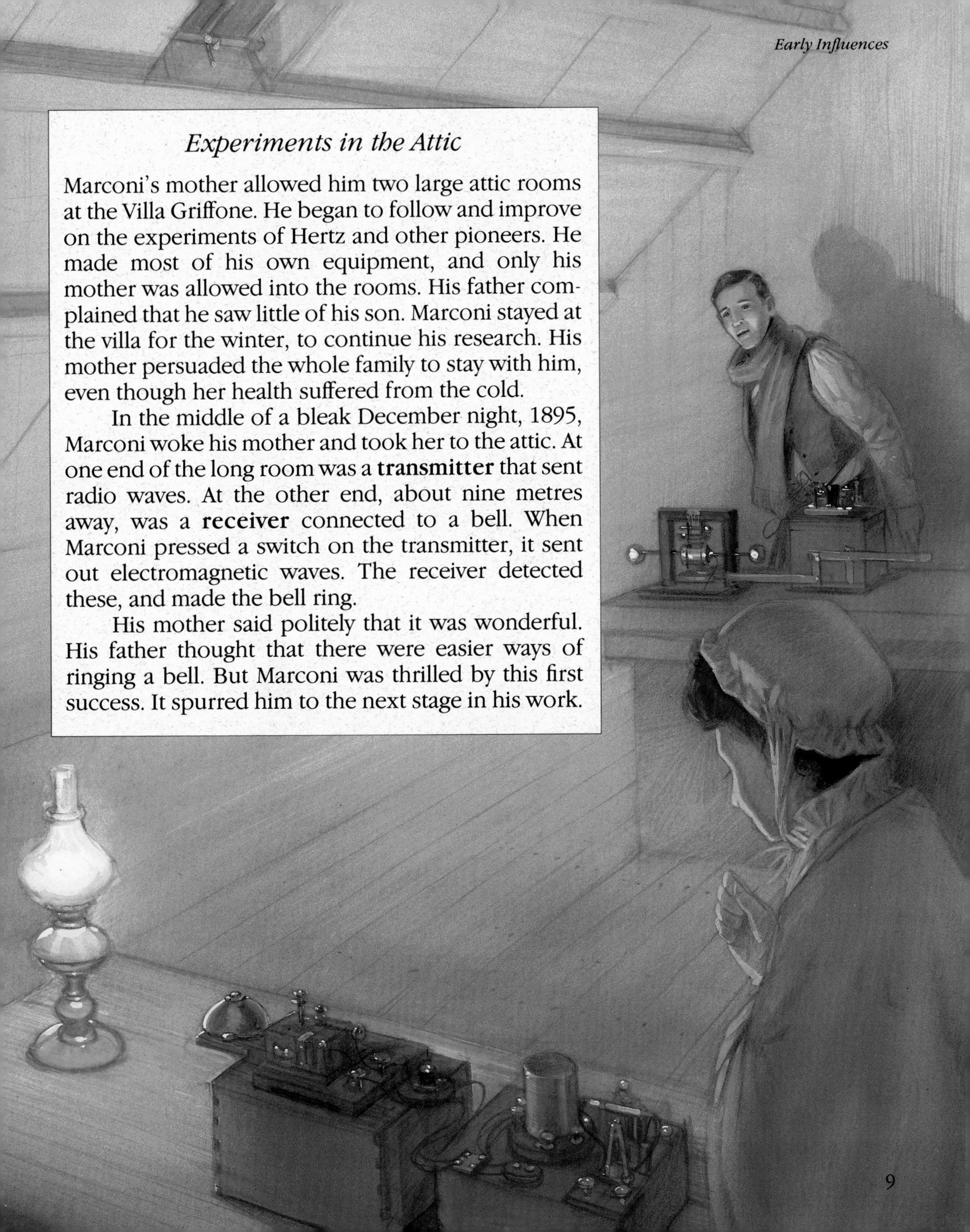

Experiments in the Attic

Marconi's mother allowed him two large attic rooms at the Villa Griffone. He began to follow and improve on the experiments of Hertz and other pioneers. He made most of his own equipment, and only his mother was allowed into the rooms. His father complained that he saw little of his son. Marconi stayed at the villa for the winter, to continue his research. His mother persuaded the whole family to stay with him, even though her health suffered from the cold.

In the middle of a bleak December night, 1895, Marconi woke his mother and took her to the attic. At one end of the long room was a **transmitter** that sent radio waves. At the other end, about nine metres away, was a **receiver** connected to a bell. When Marconi pressed a switch on the transmitter, it sent out electromagnetic waves. The receiver detected these, and made the bell ring.

His mother said politely that it was wonderful. His father thought that there were easier ways of ringing a bell. But Marconi was thrilled by this first success. It spurred him to the next stage in his work.

Chapter Two

Across the Garden

After his attic success, Marconi needed more space. He began experiments outside, among the chestnut trees of the Villa Griffone's gardens. His father still did not approve, partly because he did not believe his son's theories, and also because people kept tripping over the wires trailing around the garden.

The young Marconi, still only 22 years old, was helped by the sons of his father's workers and by his younger brother. Two of his early developments involved a more powerful transmitter and a more sensitive receiver (see panel).

With each small improvement Marconi and his team were able to detect radio waves, or Hertzian waves as they were called, from greater distances, firstly across the garden and soon even farther away. The transmitter had a sending key and the receiver worked a buzzer. In this way the team could communicate messages in the dot-dash signals of **Morse code**.

Out of Sight

At last even Guiseppe Marconi was impressed. His son's equipment, a tangle of coils and tubes and wires on poles, beamed invisible radio waves to a receiving station on the other side of a hill – out of sight! By early 1896, the transmitter and receiver were two kilometres apart.

Marconi had produced the first wireless telegraphy equipment. It could send messages in Morse code over ever-increasing distances. With more experiments and then mass production, it could have dramatic effects on the communications business.

As distances increased in the villa's grounds, Marconi and his helpers used arm-waving signals. These showed when a message was sent, and if it had been received.

Better Equipment

In a simple transmitter, a fast-oscillating electric current passed across a tiny gap, making sparks that sent out radio waves. Marconi connected one wire to a metal cylinder on a pole, and the other to a metal plate buried in the earth. The bigger sparks made stronger waves.

He also improved the **coherer**, a device already in electrical use. Electromagnetic waves made particles of carbon or metal in a tube "line up", letting an electric current pass more easily. Marconi tried different powders, tube shapes and positions, and made his receiver-coherers more sensitive.

Marconi improved the **antennas** (aerials), too. These wires radiated waves from the transmitter, and picked up waves for the receiver. Marconi tested different wire lengths, positions and patterns, and he placed them high on poles, so that the waves travelled farther.

Marconi's chief assistant George Stephen Kemp (above) stands next to radio equipment used in tests at Dover, in 1899. In Italy Marconi himself, hand on knee (in the centre, below), explains his wireless devices to officials. In the late 1890s, such demonstrations took up much of his time.

Demonstration for the Post Office

In 1896 Marconi went to London with his mother. He continued his experiments. He met William Preece, who had read about Marconi's work, and was Engineer-in-Chief at the General Post Office in London. He arranged for Marconi to demonstrate his wireless telegraphy. This he did successfully, which resulted in Preece promising Marconi his support. He also arranged for Marconi to have an assistant, George Stephen Kemp. Kemp became Marconi's life-long friend and helper until his death in 1933.

Also in 1896, Marconi obtained his first **patent** for his radio telegraphy equipment. This meant he was officially its inventor, and other people could not copy it unless Marconi gave permission.

In 1897 Marconi returned to Italy, where he gave demonstrations of his radio work to the Italian Navy, and also to King Humbert and Queen Margharita.

Marconi began to show that he had his father's business abilities. While in Italy, in July 1897, the Wireless Telegraph and Signal Company Limited was formed with his agreement, by his cousin Henry Jameson Davis in London. The company owned Marconi's patents and its aim was to develop, market and sell his inventions around the world. However, Marconi's fondness for his homeland meant that he allowed Italy to be free of patent restrictions, to develop radio equipment as it wished.

In 1900, the company became Marconi's Wireless Telegraph Company, Limited. We know its descendant today as GEC-Marconi, the giant multi-national company with interests in aerospace, defence, broadcasting, radar and satellite communications.

This photograph from 1901 (left) shows Marconi with his radio equipment, including a transmitter on his left. The paper-tape Morse printer in the middle recorded the dots and dashes of Morse code, detected by the receiver on his right. The famous physicist William Thomson, later Lord Kelvin (below), offered Marconi much help.

Farther and Farther

William Preece carried out radio tests at Dover, with the aim of sending signals across the Channel. When Marconi returned from Italy to London, Preece continued his support and encouragement.

Marconi's dream was to transmit radio waves ever farther. He continually experimented to improve his equipment. His work would have been interrupted if, like any young Italian man, he was called up to do military service.

However Marconi had new-found and influential friends, including the great scientist Lord Kelvin (1824-1907) who encouraged him for many years. In 1897, a job was arranged for him at the Italian Embassy in London, which meant he could not be called up to the army. Marconi did little work at the embassy, but continued his radio research. He still received money from home, so his embassy pay cheques went anonymously to the Italian Hospital in Bloomsbury, London.

Chapter Three

Across the Channel

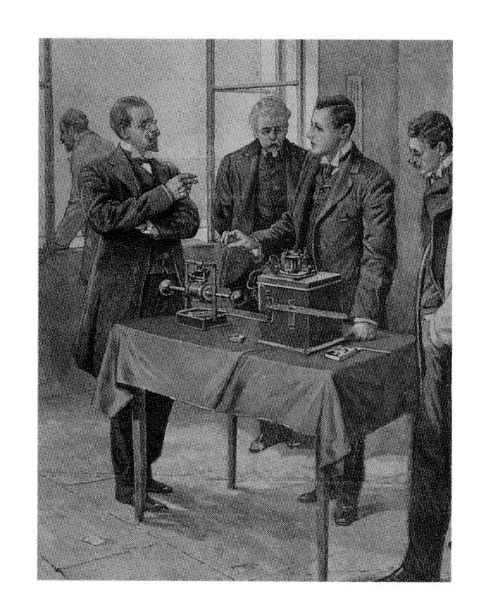

Marconi (on the right) discusses his wireless equipment.

During 1897-8, radio progressed from being an experimental curiosity, to having real uses in the real world. For example, ships could not be linked by wires to the land. Radio would enable them to send messages to each other and to radio stations on the shore. Therefore many experiments were done around the British coast.

A radio station was set up at Alum Bay on the Isle of Wight, with aerial masts 37 metres tall. Another at Bournemouth was later moved to Poole.

The First News by Radio

In 1898 Marconi's company was asked to set up a radio system on the north coast of Ireland. They installed a radio station at a lighthouse on Rathlin Island, off Ballycastle, and another at Ballycastle. Information about ships passing the island could then be sent to the mainland.

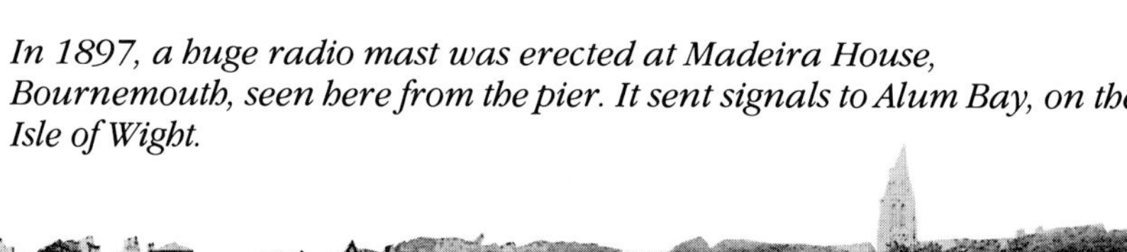

In 1897, a huge radio mast was erected at Madeira House, Bournemouth, seen here from the pier. It sent signals to Alum Bay, on the Isle of Wight.

Marconi sent news of yacht races from a radio room on board a boat.

In July 1898, the Irish *Dublin Express* was the first newspaper to gather news by radio. At a yacht race in the Irish Sea, part of the Kingstown Regatta, the reporter was Marconi himself. He followed the yachts in a tugboat, and radioed news to a receiving station at Kingstown. The reports were sent on to Dublin by telephone.

Marconi said of this event: "Previously it had been the more scientifically-minded who were interested [in wireless]. Now, the man in the street began to wonder whether this wireless might not be of use to him."

Tales of Black Magic

Work continued at Alum Bay on the Isle of Wight. The tall mast was a mystery and wonder to local people. Those who entered the test buildings saw sparks longer than their hands, glowing in the darkness. Sometimes strange kites carried aerial wires to great heights. The popular newspapers wrote about tales of "black magic".

Few people, even other scientists, understood the true nature of radio waves. Marconi knew that they were largely unaffected by clouds, wind, fog, and the darkness of night. But many of his colleagues still thought that the mysterious waves could not travel through bad weather.

Tuning the Radio

Receivers that detected a wide range of radio waves produced a muddled mix of sounds. So Marconi worked on the principle of tuning a transmitter and receiver to certain frequencies. The frequency, in Hertz (page 8), is the number of waves in one second, shown in the diagram. As frequency increases, wavelength decreases. Most radio signals have frequencies of 30,000 Hz to 300,000 million Hz.

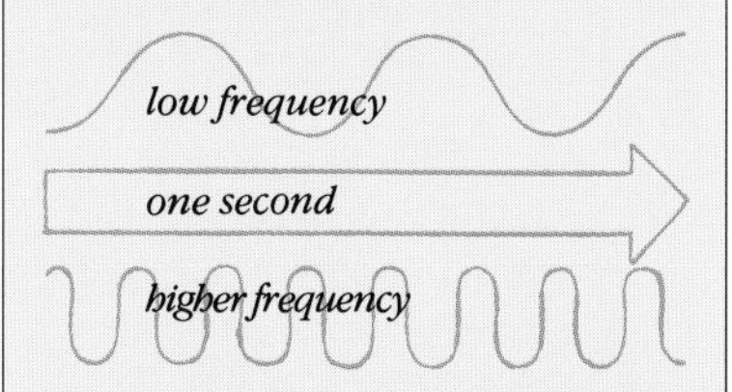

Marconi adjusted the electrical circuits of transmitter and receiver to a very narrow range of frequencies. This improved the reception quality, since interfering radio signals of other frequencies were not picked up. It also helped the armed forces, who were worried about other people picking up secret messages. Now the forces could use their own, secret frequency.

Today, we tune radio and TV sets to various "broadcast" channels or stations. For example, Britain's Radio 1 is 97-99 Mhz (million Hertz).

The Queen and the Prince's Knee

The Prince of Wales (above) enjoyed yachting, and after Marconi's demonstrations, he encouraged the Navy to take up wireless equipment. In 1899 the East Goodwin lightship (below) was involved in one of the first radio rescues.

In 1898, while Queen Victoria was staying at Osborne House on the Isle of Wight, the Prince of Wales (later Edward VII) injured his knee. He chose to stay on the Royal Yacht *Osborne*. Marconi was asked to install radio equipment on the Royal Yacht and at Osborne House. This he did, and he took the opportunity to carry out more distance experiments, as the yacht sailed around the island and the Prince followed the Cowes Regatta.

The Queen and the Prince exchanged about 150 messages by radio over 16 days, with no problems. The eminent newspaper *The Times* even reported some of them. Marconi was proud to be summoned to see Queen Victoria. She wished him many further successes. The Prince became very keen on the technical side of radio and agreed that "electrical waves through the ether" had a great future. Navy warships were soon being fitted with radio equipment.

On 3 March 1899, a steamship became stuck on the treacherous Goodwin Sands, near Dover. The East Goodwin lightship sent radio messages to the mainland and the lifeboats were launched. The entire crew and more than £50,000 worth of cargo were rescued. Radio had saved lives, and Marconi was very pleased.

Radio across the Channel

The Queen's interest, and reports in the newspapers, meant that Marconi and his "wireless telegraphy" became ever more famous. Their fame increased still further with the development of cross-Channel radio signals. The first messages between France and England were sent in March 1899, from a radio station at Wimereux, near Boulogne. They were received 51 kilometres away at South Foreland, near Dover. French government officials were very impressed, and at once they arranged radio equipment for their armed forces.

Marconi was already planning the next stage in his work. He wanted to beam radio waves across a much wider stretch of water – the Atlantic Ocean.

A Strange Silence

After the first cross-Channel radio signals, Marconi stayed for a time at Wimereux. He worked alongside his men on the electrical equipment, building repairs and other odd jobs.

Famous people visited. One was General Baden Powell (1857-1941), soldier and founder of the Scouting movement. Marconi was eager to show his equipment. At 10 pm one evening, he tapped the Morse key and sent a message to England. No reply. He tried again. Nothing. He and Baden Powell checked the wires and connections, even outside in the rainstorm. Marconi was embarrassed, and began to lose faith in his work. Had his ideas about radio been wrong?

Suddenly the receiver and Morse equipment jumped into life. It was a message from England: "Just back from supper, anything happening your end?"

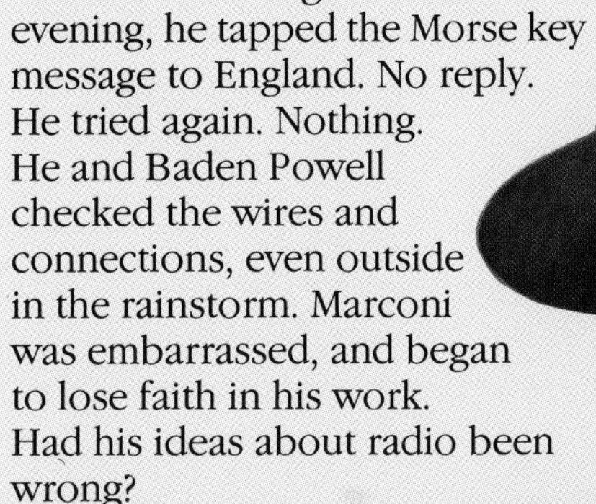

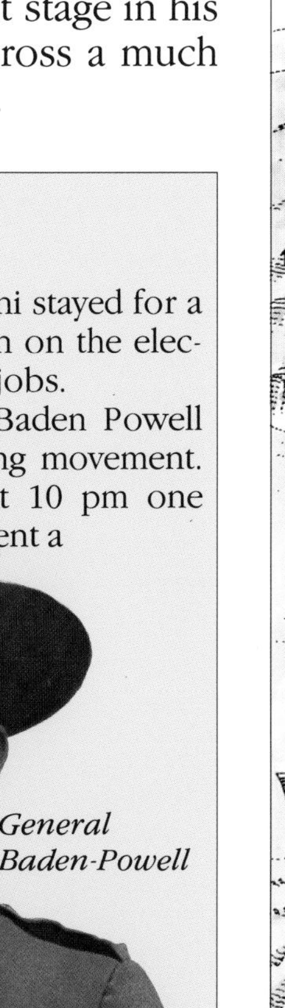

General Baden-Powell

Linking Countries

Wireless signals crossed the Channel in 1899. Both stations were high up on the coast, so that the radio waves could travel further.

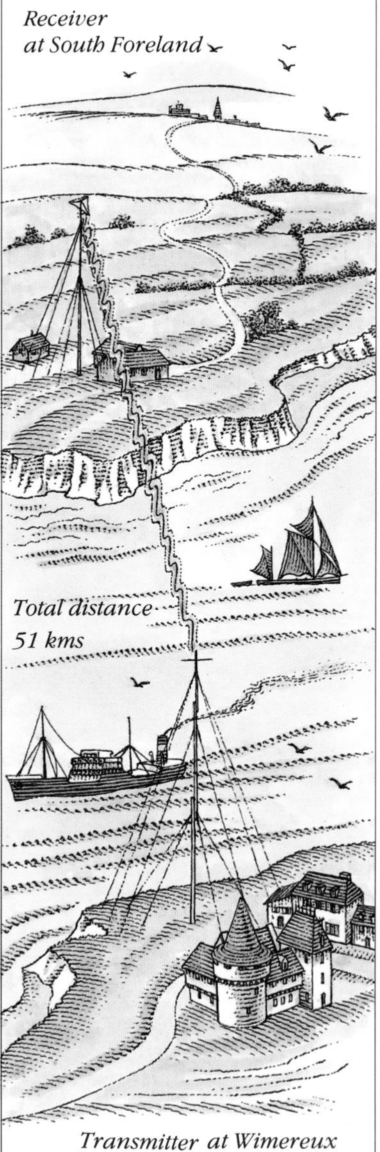

Chapter Four

Across the Atlantic

During 1899, Marconi and his teams worked steadily on radio improvements. The Italian inventor was still only 25 years old, yet his fame spread far and wide. His work was continually interrupted as he was asked to give demonstrations as far apart as Australia, Brazil and China.

In 1900 Marconi patented improvements for transmitters and receivers to use new combinations of tuning, and a single aerial to send and receive many radio messages of more than one frequency. It was patent number 7777, which was later challenged by other radio companies (page 22).

Marconi's thoughts were still on radio signals across the Atlantic. In July 1900 he visited the far west of England and selected a site at Poldhu, Cornwall, for his most powerful radio station yet built. It was tested during early 1901 and sent messages more than 300 kilometres.

A receiving station was then built at Saint John's, Newfoundland, more than 2,700 kilometres across the ocean. Marconi and his assistants set up their equipment on nearby Signal Hill, using kites and balloons to try and hold up the aerial wires in the windswept conditions.

The radio station at Poldhu, Cornwall was a forest of immense masts (above). It sent long-wave signals, which need far more power than shorter wavelengths.

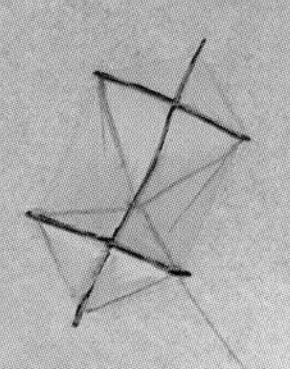

"S" for Success

The great day came on 12 December 1901. Marconi had sent messages back to England by the under-ocean telegraph cable, telling the Poldhu transmitter to send radio signals between 12 noon and 3 pm local time.

At about 12.30 pm, Marconi heard three faint clicks in the telephone connected to the radio receiver. Then again, and again. It was morse code for the letter "S" – the message they had chosen because it was short and easy to send, yet recognizable. Kemp heard it too. The signals came all the way from England. Radio had bridged the Atlantic.

The news startled and surprised many people. Even the great inventor Thomas Edison (1847-1931), an admirer and friend of Marconi, asked if they had perhaps picked up stray signals. Others believed that the Earth's curved surface would prevent the radio waves travelling such long distances (see panel on page 21).

The station at Signal Hill was based around an old military barracks. Marconi's diary records that radio signals were first received at 12.30, 1.10 and 2.30 pm on Thursday 12 December. The Atlantic had been bridged!

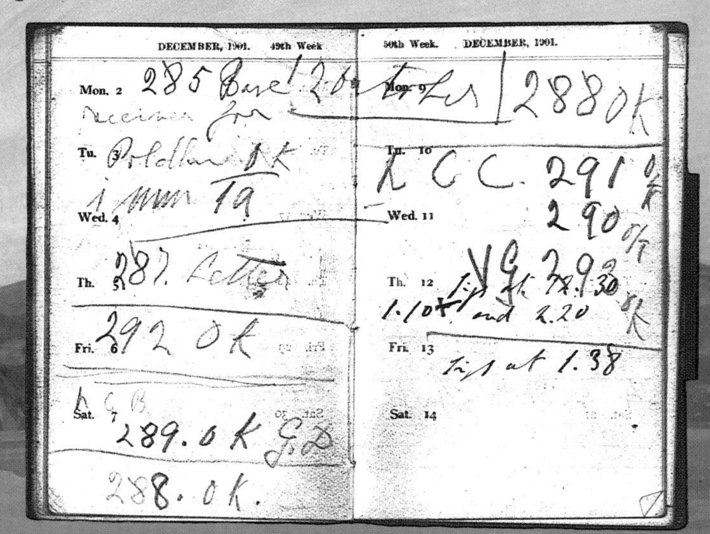

DECEMBER, 1901. 49th Week

Mon. 2 285
Tu. 3 Poldhu OK
Wed. 4
Th. 5 287
Fri. 6 292 OK
Sat. 7 289. OK
288. OK.

50th Week. DECEMBER, 1901.

Mon. 9 288 OK
Tu. 10 291 OK
Wed. 11 290 OK
Th. 12 293 OK
1.10 and 2.20
Fri. 13 at 1.38
Sat. 14

Marconi's double-spark-gap apparatus.

Greater Power

Marconi and his team knew there would be technical problems in sending radio signals vast distances across the Atlantic. They had to produce a spark 5 centimetres long, and very powerful. Marconi's colleague Professor Ambrose Fleming designed a double-transformer in which the electrical power was stepped up, then stepped up again to tremendously high voltage, before reaching the aerial.

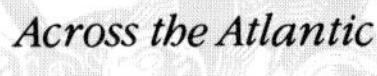

Radio engineers try to launch a large kite at Signal Hill, Saint John's. The kite pulled aloft dozens of metres of radio aerial wire. Marconi looks on from the left.

Marconi had to be dressed for cold weather in Newfoundland, during the winter of 1901-2. Signal Hill was cold, wet and windy, with fog and driving rain.

Problems and Patents

Almost at once, the Anglo-American Telegraph Company threatened Marconi with **legal action**, saying that it alone was permitted to carry out telegraphy, wired or wireless, in Newfoundland (then under British control). Marconi moved his station to Glace Bay, Nova Scotia, Canada, and carried on his trans-Atlantic tests there.

The event marked a period of long, expensive patent battles. Other companies were jealous of Marconi's success, and the fact that they could only copy his equipment with permission, and usually with money payments, too.

Making Radio Reliable

In 1902, Marconi was saddened by the death of his father Guiseppe. But, as ever, he busied himself with research. At the radio station in Glace Bay, the signals received from Cornwall were faint and unpredictable. Marconi knew that unless they improved, people would continue to use the under-ocean telegraph cable.

In his determined manner, Marconi set to work on the equipment, and encouraged his colleagues. They improved the system. By the beginning of 1903 signals were beamed reliably between Glace Bay and Poldhu. Among the first batch were personal thank-you messages from Marconi to the Kings Edward VII of Great Britain and Victor Emmanuel III of Italy, who had succeeded his father in 1900. Marconi was always polite – and keen to keep in their good favour.

Radio around the Globe

Some scientists believed Marconi could not send radio signals across the Atlantic. Electromagnetic waves travel in straight lines and cannot travel far through the ground. It was thought they would either be absorbed by the curve of the Earth's surface or radiated off into space.

However, signals do cross the Atlantic. Firstly, the Earth's surface tends to reflect radio waves rather than absorb them. Travelling out to space, the waves encounter a second reflective surface, the **ionosphere**. This is a layer high up around the Earth where some matter exists as **ions** rather than normal **atoms**. It reflects radio waves in the same way a curved mirror reflects light. Signals cross the Atlantic by bouncing up and down in a zig-zag pattern between the ionosphere and the Earth's surface many times.

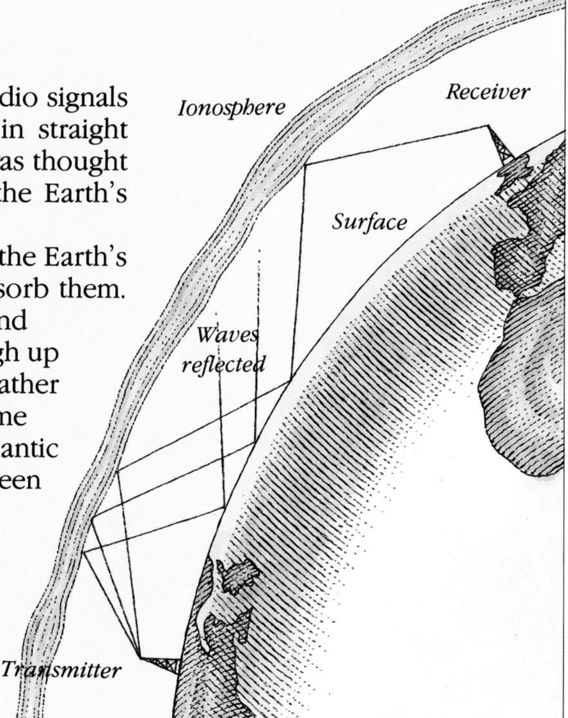

The ionosphere reflects radio waves as they bounce up and down, around the curved surface of the Earth.

A Meeting of Minds

During 1903 radio links were being set up through Europe, between Denmark and Iceland, and in Russia. There were plans for a link between Australia and New Zealand, and radio stations in many other places around the world.

There were still doubts and criticisms about Marconi's scientific work. Patent battles dragged on. But Marconi continued his research, and answered his opponents by better and better results.

On his next business visit to the USA, he visited Thomas Edison, who had developed the light bulb, electricity supply network, and many other devices. These two men, whose inventions changed everyday life for ever, had tremendous respect and admiration for each other. They talked for hours. Edison said that the world would scarcely be capable of realizing all that Marconi had done.

Inventor Thomas Edison (1847-1931) admired Marconi's achievements.

A Voice on the Radio

In 1906 US physicist Reginald Fessenden (1866-1932) transmitted music and voice clearly by radio, for the first time. He used the AM technique (see page 25). Previous transmissions had been telegraphic, that is, the stop-starts of Morse code. Fessenden sent his voice and Handel's music by radio waves to ships in the Atlantic Ocean.

Chapter Five

Around the World

Marconi's ultimate ambition was to see a network of radio stations linking all parts of the world. In 1908, his English company began to send public messages between Britain, Canada and the USA. Radio stations were established in Australia, and the next year in India.

Meanwhile radio equipment became increasingly powerful, sensitive and reliable, and less expensive. One great advance was the **triode valve**, devised by Lee de Forest (1873-1961). It could amplify, or make bigger, tiny electrical currents such as those produced by radio receivers. Previously the only electricity made by a receiver came from the effects of the radio waves on the antenna. The amounts were small, barely enough to work the earpiece of a headphone. With the triode, these signals could be amplified to power loudspeakers at high volume, so that many people could listen.

1909 saw a great honour for Marconi. He was awarded the Nobel Prize for Physics, along with Karl Ferdinand Braun (1850-1918), for their great contributions to wireless telegraphy.

There followed another legal battle, over the famous patent 7777. For the first time radio was used inside a court of law, for demonstration purposes. Marconi won, and proved that he was truly the "Father of Radio".

Marconi was always trying new ideas for radio. Here, he attends tests of a mobile radio van in Milan, Italy in 1906.

Success and Scandal

The year of 1912 was mixed. Marconi House opened in London. New regulations said that large ships must have radios, and these must be continually manned. But in September Marconi lost an eye in a car accident in Italy.

The next year saw the "Marconi Company Scandal". People said Marconi had a secret, unfair agreement with the British government to establish chains of radio stations. There was uproar and more legal problems.

In 1914 the Marconi-Bellini-Tosi Apparatus for finding ships in foggy weather was first used. Less happily, World War One began. Radio was banned in England, except with official permission. Marconi returned to Italy and played an active role in war, in charge of wireless telegraphy for the army.

By 1918 the war was over. Marconi began experiments on transmitting the human voice by radio. A radio link between England and Australia was established. At last, radio truly circled the globe.

Radio enters Daily Life

During the early 1900s, radio was having more effect on the daily lives of ordinary people, especially by communicating news.

- In 1910 news of King Edward VII's death was sent out by radio.
- In the same year, Doctor Crippen was arrested on the liner *Montrose* off the Canadian coast, as the ship approached North America. He was trying to escape to America after murdering his wife – the first criminal caught by radio.
- In 1912 the "unsinkable" liner *Titanic* hit an iceberg off Newfoundland on her first voyage. She sank, and 1,500 people died. But radio was responsible for bringing rescue ships to save 700 other passengers and crew.

Titanic *disaster.*

Le Petit Journal

SUPPLEMENT ILLUSTRÉ

DIMANCHE 14 AOUT 1910

ARRESTATION DU DOCTEUR CRIPPEN ET DE MISS LE NEVE SUR LE PONT DU «MONTROSE»

Crippen is arrested!

Marconi's steam-powered yacht Elettra *was 72 metres long and weighed 700 tonnes. For many years it was his floating house, laboratory, workshop, and mobile radio station. He carried out innumerable tests from its Wireless Room (right).*

In 1920 Marconi's mother died. She had never ceased her support and encouragement, and he felt great sorrow.

Marconi kept the home in Italy. In 1919 he had bought a yacht, *Elettra*, as a travelling laboratory. He wanted to spend more time at sea, away from public attention. Kings, Queens, politicians and scientists visited him on his floating home.

In 1926 Marconi returned in triumph to his home town of Bologna on the 30th anniversary of his first radio patent. Crowds cheered madly, and restaurants served "spaghetti à la Marconi" and "Wireless pasta".

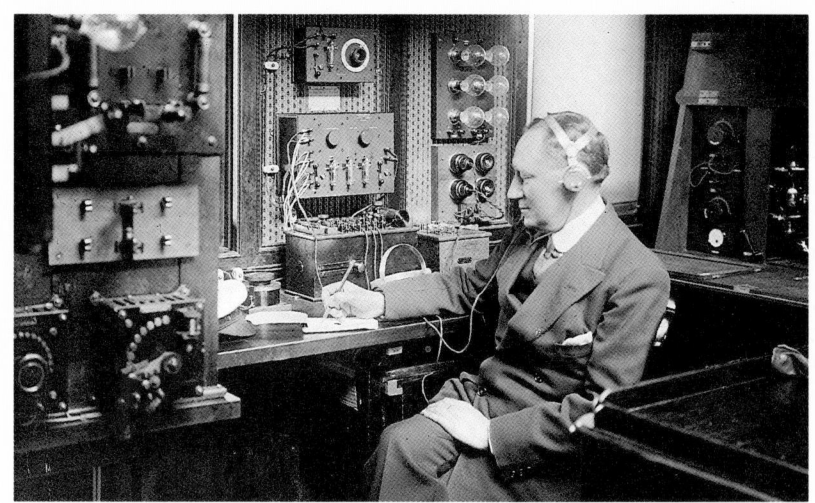

The Marconis relax on board the Elettra. *He valued the yacht as a quiet retreat, where he could "study and experiment without the fear of unwelcome interruption."*

Marconi the Man

Marconi had married Beatrice O'Brien in 1905. They had three children together but divorced in 1924. In 1927 Marconi married 23-year-old Countess Maria Cristina Bezzi Scala in Rome. They agreed to live aboard the yacht and keep a country home near Rome.

Marconi was an active sportsman. He was also a good businessman. At work or play, he could not be rushed, and paid great attention to detail. He had a sense of humour and was described as "an agreeable companion". He always remained an Italian citizen, but he loved Britain and liked to visit his mother's homeland in Ireland.

Most of all, he was very determined and single-minded, especially about radio. From 1924 he began work on beam radio systems, which sent out focused beams of short-wave radio in one direction only, rather than in all directions. The signals carried more information with less interference. In 1928 he began work on beam transmitters that could turn around, to direct the beamed waves to different places in turn.

A Fitting Tribute

Awards and honours flooded in. Marconi was created an hereditary Marquis of Italy. The Pope awarded him the Grand Cross of the Order of Pius XI. This meant a great deal to Marconi, who was a religious man.

In 1930 the Marconis had a daughter, Elettra. The family cruised the globe on their yacht of the same name, visiting radio stations and being honoured by world leaders. Marconi's health had always been fairly good. However, a severe heart condition (diagnosed in 1927) led to several heart attacks in the 1930s. He continued to work despite this, although he ceased to travel out of Italy, except aboard the *Elettra.*

Guglielmo Marconi died in Rome on 20 July 1937 after a major heart attack. In an astonishing tribute during his funeral, radio stations around the world went silent for two minutes in his honour.

Marconi was often asked: "Have you had any signals from Mars?" His reply was: "I am concerned enough at present with business upon Earth."

AM to FM Radio

Speech and music consist of varying sound waves. To send them by radio, these sound patterns must be turned into patterns of electrical signals, and then into patterns of varying radio waves that carry the same information.

AM – amplitude (height) varies

AM Early systems, as used by Reginald Fessenden in his pioneer broadcasts, varied the height or amplitude of the radio waves. This is amplitude modulation, AM. It is still used for radio broadcast on short, medium and long waves.

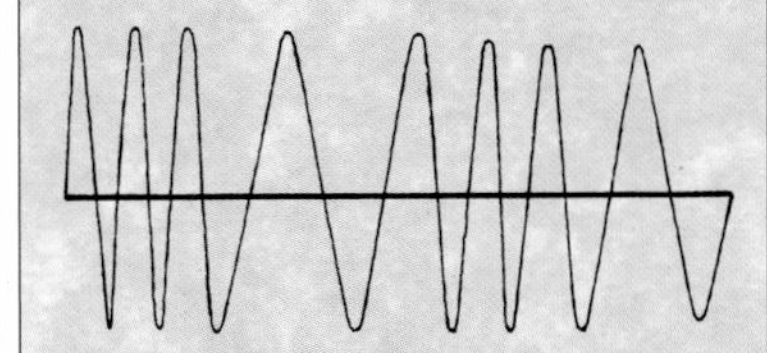

FM – frequency varies

FM From 1925, Edwin Armstrong (1890-1954) devised a system to carry the information by varying the wave frequency. This is frequency modulation, FM. It cuts out most of the natural interference and hiss. Today's high-quality radio broadcasts use FM.

Chapter Six

After Marconi

Marconi's working life is almost a history of the main events at the start of our century. This shows the importance of radio's impact on the world, in news-gathering, radio broadcasting and military communications.

The first regular radio broadcasts were made in early 1920s. The years from 1925 to 1950 are sometimes called the "Heyday of Radio". News programmes, variety shows, music, drama and interviews filled the airwaves. By the 1930s radio was in common use by the police and armed forces, and the expanding passenger airlines.

Televisions began to invade homes in the 1950s. The TV set receives a complex modulated radio wave carrying both sound and vision signals.

From Sound to Vision

In the 1950-60s television began to take over from radio, though TV also uses what we call radio waves. In 1931 Marconi was asked if he thought television, then in its early stages, would become as common as radio. He replied: "Yes . . . I am not sure that television will ever be in such general use as radio broadcasting is today . . . Certainly I think the day will come when we shall be able to see one another whilst talking as we are now." TV has become part of daily life, though the two-way system Marconi mentioned is far from commonplace.

Each invention is judged against the technology of the age. Early "portable" radios were regarded as miraculous inventions. Research has since brought transistors and silicon-based microcircuits. The same equipment now fits in the palm of the hand.

Seeing with radio: the radar displays at an Air Traffic Control centre.

During World War Two (1939-45) there were many developments in radio and also radar, which stands for **ra**dio **d**etection **a**nd **r**anging. Radio waves are beamed out, and their reflections or echoes picked up by a sensitive receiver. This system identifies planes, ships and other objects. It is now an essential tool for the armed forces, ships and planes, and air traffic controllers.

Today, invisible radio waves are everywhere we look: television, hi-fi tuners, portable radios, car radios, space communications, radio astronomy, tiny radio-microphones and "bugs" used by performers and spies, walkie-talkies, even radio-controlled models and automatic-opening garage doors. Marconi and his fellow scientists made essential contributions to our Wire-less World.

Footnote

Different countries have different views about inventors, especially in a subject such as radio, which involved the work of many people. After Hertz and before Marconi, Russian physicist Alexander Popov (1859-1906) transmitted the words "Heinrich Hertz" in Morse code by radio, as a demonstration for the Russian Chemical Society. In Russia Popov, not Marconi, is sometimes known as the "Father of Radio".

Microwaves

Toward the end of his research, Marconi became interested in microwaves. These are electromagnetic in nature, like radio waves. But they have shorter wavelengths, from about 30 centimetres down to 1 millimetre. Marconi predicted that this "hitherto unexplored range of electrical waves" would be useful for short-distance communication, and "it is difficult to tell yet in what new fields they may be applied".

Today, microwaves are used in many ways, including radar. They carry television programmes between land stations about 40 kilometres apart, and beam signals to and from orbiting satellites. Marconi would probably be most amazed as microwaves defrost and cook food, in a microwave oven.

A modern TV studio, less than 100 years after Marconi's first experiments in Villa Griffone's attic.

The World in Marconi's Time

	1850-1875	1876-1900
Science	**1859** Gaston Planté invents the rechargeable battery **1861** The telegraph line connects New York and San Francisco for the first time **1874** Marconi is born	**1879** Thomas Edison in the USA and Joseph Swan in England separately invent the first light bulbs **1884** Lewis Waterman invents the Fountain pen **1897** Alexander Popov in Russia transmits radio waves over five kilometres
Exploration	**1859** Ferdinand de Lesseps digs the first shovel of earth for the Suez Canal. It takes ten years to build **1864** Samuel Baker travels down the Nile and shows that the river flows through Lake Albert Nyanza	**1879** Nikolay Przhevalsky (Przewalski) identifies the last truly wild horses, changed little since prehistoric times in Central Asia **1891** Construction of Trans-Siberian railway begins
Politics	**1863** Slavery is abolished in the USA, during the American Civil War **1868** Labrador becomes part of Canada **1871** Rome becomes the capital of the newly united Italy	**1877** The Satsuma rebellion in Japan helps to close the age-old tradition of Samurai power **1885** In Sudan, Africa, the Siege of Khartoum ends with the death of General Gordon **1886** Germany and Britain partition East Africa
Art	**1858** Jacques Offenbach completes his lively operetta *Orpheus in the Underworld* **1871** Claude Monet, a founder of impressionism, paints *Houses of Parliament seen from Westminster Bridge* in London **1875** Mark Twain publishes *Tom Sawyer*	**1877** First performance of the ballet *Swan Lake* by Peter Tchaikovsky **1883** London's Royal College of Music comes into being **1885** William Gilbert and Arthur Sullivan complete their light opera *The Mikado*

1901-1925	1926-1950
1901 The first Nobel Prize for Physics is awarded to Wilhelm Rontgen, for the discovery of X-rays	**1928** First general use of radio beacons for ship and plane navigation
1909 Nobel Prize for Physics awarded jointly to Marconi and Karl Braun	**1932** James Chadwick announces that he has detected the sub-atomic particle, the neutron
	1937 Marconi dies
1909 Robert Peary is supposed to be the first person to reach the North Pole, though some doubts have been cast on this claim over the years	**1946-7** Massive US expedition photographs over half the coastline of Antarctica
1922 Tomb of Tutankhamen discovered at Luxor	
1908 Manchu power in China ends, soon followed by revolution	**1929** The Wall Street Crash in the American Business world
1914 World War One begins	**1939** World War Two begins
1917 Nobel Prize for Peace awarded to the International Red Cross Committee	**1944** Nobel Prize for Peace again awarded to the International Red Cross Committee
1918 World War One ends	**1945** World War Two ends
1910 Forster completes his novel *Howard's End*	**1929** Salvador Dali, leader of the surrealist movement, has his first exhibition of paintings
1911 The tango, a dance from South America, becomes popular in North America and Europe	**1935** Singer Elvis Presley born in Tupelo, Mississippi, USA
1913 Charles Chaplin makes his first short film	**1936** Britain begins the first regular public television transmissions

Glossary

alternating current: an *electric current* that flows first one way then the other, often millions of times each second (in electricity found in a house, 50 or 60 times each second).

antenna: in radio, the aerial which sends or receives signals. It may be a wire, rod, dish, grid or other shape.

atoms: the smallest parts of a substance, far too tiny to see under the most powerful microscope. Atoms can be split into smaller particles, such as electrons and neutrons, but these no longer have the physical and chemical features of the original substance.

battery: *see* cell.

cell: in electrical work, a device containing various chemicals that produces a flow of electricity. More accurately, a single device like this is called a cell, and two or more linked together are a battery.

coherer: an electrical device in which particles line up or cling to each other, under the influence of electromagnetic waves, electricity or magnetism.

electric current: a flow of electricity through a substance, for example through a metal wire.

electromagnetic waves: waves having features of both electricity and magnetism, that can travel through air, space and many substances.

etheric: of the "ether". In the past this was thought to be an unseen, undetectable substance which was present everywhere. Its existence has been proposed for various reasons, such as carrying light rays or magnetism. However modern science no longer accepts the existence of an ether.

frequency: the number of times something happens. In *electromagnetic waves* it is the number of complete waves in one second. If an electromagnetic wave has a high frequency, then its *wavelength* is short.

induction coils: in electrical work, coils of wire used for greatly increasing the voltage or "strength" of an **electric current**.

ionosphere: a layer high above the Earth, where *ions* are much more common than in the normal atmosphere.

ions: *atoms* which have a positive or negative electrical charge, rather than the usual neutral state (no charge).

legal action: using the laws and rules of the country to show that someone has done something illegal (against the law).

magnetic field: an area or field of a magnetic force, in which a magnet exerts its *magnetism.*

magnetism: a still-mysterious force, produced by a magnet or a *electric current,* which can attract, repel or change substances at a distance.

Morse code: a code of short electrical signals (dots) and long ones (dashes), that spell out letters and words. For example, the letter S is dot-dot-dot. The code was invented by American Samuel Morse in about 1838, for use on the telegraph system.

patent: a legal document showing that someone is the official inventor of a device or product and has the sole right to make and sell it, for a time period. Others can do so only with permission of the patent holder.

radar: RAdio Detection And Ranging. Beaming radio waves at an object and analyzing their bounced-back "echoes" to find the object's position and direction.

radio waves: types of *electromagnetic waves* used for conveying information in radio, television, radar and similar applications. They have *wavelengths* of many kilometres down to about one metre.

radio-astronomy telescopes: telescopes that look into space and receive radio waves, rather than the usual light rays of the optical telescope.

receiver: the part of a radio system that detects radio waves and turns them into electrical signals.

satellite communications: using the man-made satellites that circle the Earth to communicate and send messages, usually by radio waves and microwaves.

transformer: in electrical work, a device with two or more coils of wire, that changes the "strength" (voltage) of an *alternating current.*

transmitter: the part of a radio system that takes electrical signals and sends them out as radio waves.

triode valve: an electrical device, with three parts or electrodes, for amplifying (making bigger) electrical signals.

wavelength: the distance from a point on one wave, such as the highest part or peak, to the same point on the next wave. It can be on any wave, from radio to ocean.

Index